© John Tully 1979

Printed and published in Great Britain by
William Collins Sons and Co Ltd
Glasgow G4 0NB

All rights reserved. No part of this book may be reproduced,
stored in a retrieval system, or transmitted in any form or by
any means, electronic, mechanical, photocopying, recording
or otherwise, without the prior permission of the Publisher.

First published in Collins English Library, 1979

4 5 6 7 8 9 10

Collins English Library   Level 2

An Inspector Holt Story
THE BRIDGE
JOHN TULLY

Illustrations by Maureen and Gordon Gray

Collins: London and Glasgow

Chapter 1

It was Sunday afternoon. The street was quiet. A young Arab, Hassan, walked towards the house where he lived.

Two men jumped out from behind a wall. One was tall with long black hair. The other man was shorter, but heavy and strong. The tall man put a coat over Hassan's head. The other took hold of his arms. Hassan fought but he could not get free.

A police car came into the street. Bill Ojo was the driver. Inspector Holt was beside him.

Bill saw the two men with Hassan. "Look! Look there!"

The tall man put Hassan into the back of a red motor car and climbed in after him. The shorter man got into the driver's seat. The car moved off.

"After them!" said Holt.

Bill drove fast after the other car.

The tall man saw the police car behind them. "Faster!" he said to his friend. They turned into another street. There were more cars in this street, and buses. The driver turned from side to side to get past them. He could not go fast enough. The police car came closer.

"Get in front of them if you can," said Holt.

Bill saw an open space. He put his foot down hard. The police car shot round the other one – then slowed down in front of it.

The red car stopped. The tall man and the short one both jumped out. They ran off down a side street. Hassan was still inside with the coat over his head.

Bill ran into the side street. He could not see the two men. He went into a shop, but they were not there. He tried another shop, and another.

At last he went back to Holt. "No good," he said. "They've escaped."

Holt and Bill took Hassan to the Police Station.

"Do you know those men?" asked Holt.

"I didn't see their faces," said Hassan.

"Why did they try to take you away?"

"I don't know that either. Perhaps they wanted money."

"Money? From you?"

"Not from me. From my father, Sheik Rahman. He's a rich man. He would pay a lot of money to get me back."

"What are you doing in England?" asked Bill.

"I came here to learn engineering. How to build bridges – that kind of thing. I've learnt all I can here. I'm flying back home tomorrow. I'm going to work at a new bridge they're building. It's the Khabur Bridge."

"We'll send a man with you to the airport," said Holt.

"Thank you," said Hassan. "Will you find those men?"

"We'll try," said Holt.

Police looked for the men but didn't find them. Hassan flew back home. Three days later Holt and Bill went to see the Chief of Police.

"About those two men," said the Chief. "We think they've left the country."

"Good," said Holt.

"It's not good," said the Chief. "We think they've followed Hassan. We've told his father about it. Sheik Rahman is afraid. He thinks they'll try to take his son away again."

"We can't do much about that," said Bill.

"Oh yes, you can! Only two people have seen those men. You, Inspector, and you, Ojo. Sheik Rahman wants you to help him."

"How can we help?" asked Holt.

"You can go to his country for two weeks."

"Us?" said Bill.

"Yes, both of you. See that Hassan is all right. And find those men. You're good at that. You always find people when you want to."

"We do in England, perhaps," said Holt.

"Now you can do it in the Middle East," said the Chief. "Have a good time."

Chapter 2

Holt and Bill came out of the airport.

"It's hot here," said Holt.

"Yes," said Bill. "I like it."

"All right for you!"

A small man with a brown face came up to them. "Are you Mr Holt and Mr Ojo?" he asked.

"That's us," said Holt.

"My name is Ahmed. I've come to meet you. This way, please."

He led them to a large car which belonged to Sheik Rahman. Holt and Bill got in. Ahmed drove them to the city. He stopped at a big hotel.

"You'll stay at this hotel. Your rooms are ready for you."

"How much will it cost?" asked Holt.

"It will cost you nothing. Sheik Rahman will pay."

"I like it more and more," said Bill.

"I'll come back when you've eaten," said

Ahmed. "The Sheik will meet you this afternoon."

Holt and Bill went to their rooms. They put their clothes away. Holt had some papers and notes which he put in a desk. He put some money in the desk too, and shut it.

They had a meal at the hotel. Then Ahmed came back with the car. He drove them through the city to a big white house. They passed through an open space in the middle of the house. Here there was a garden with bright flowers. On the other side was a big room coloured blue and gold.

"Wait here," said Ahmed.

He went out. In a little while Sheik Rahman came into the room. Another man was with him.

"I'm very pleased to see you," said the Sheik. "This is Captain Salem, our Commissioner of Police."

"How do you do?" said Holt.

"I'll help you in any way I can," said Salem.

"I'm very much afraid for my son," said the Sheik.

"Where is Hassan now?"

"He's working at the Khabur Bridge. We're building a new railway from the mountains down to the sea. It crosses the Khabur River. We're building a bridge there. It's nearly finished now. Hassan is working with the Chief Engineer, Mr Scott. He's learning about the bridge, how they build it."

"I'd like to talk to him again," said Holt. "Can we go to the bridge?"

"Of course," said the Sheik. "Ahmed will bring the car for you tomorrow morning."

Holt and Bill left the house with Salem. They had dinner with him and talked for a long time. It was late when they got back to their hotel.

Holt went to his room and found the door open. He went to the desk. That was open too. His money was still there but there were no papers. He called Bill into the room.

"A thief has taken my papers but not the money. So he knew what he wanted. They were my notes about Hassan."

"Those two men, perhaps?" said Bill.

"Or others working with them. How did they know we were here?"

"There's more to this than we thought," said Bill.

Ahmed drove them out of the city towards the mountains. Bill sat in front with Ahmed. Holt sat in the back, writing out his notes again.

There were cars, buses and lorries on the road. Bill saw a big, heavy lorry coming towards them. As it came closer Bill saw the driver's face.

"That driver is looking at us all the time," said Bill. "Why does he want to....?"

Then the lorry turned across the road, towards them.

"Look out!" cried Bill.

Ahmed turned the wheel, but too late. The car turned over as the lorry crashed into it. The heavy lorry didn't stop. It went on fast, down the road.

The car fell off the road into a field. It landed on its side.

Chapter 3

Bill found Ahmed on top of him.

"Are you hurt?" asked Ahmed.

"Not badly," said Bill. He turned to Holt at the back. "Are you all right?"

"No, I'm not," said Holt. "I've lost my notes again."

They climbed out of the car.

"What happened?" asked Holt.

"A man drove his lorry into us," said Bill. "He wanted to kill us!"

A large black car stopped beside them and a man got out. He was heavily built with a round face like a full moon. "Can I help you?" he asked.

"We're going to the Khabur Bridge," said Holt. "Can you take us that way?"

"Of course," said the stranger. "But you must come home with me first. Sit down and have a drink. You'll feel better then. My name is Kossoff. Vladimir Kossoff."

"Pleased to meet you," said Holt.

Kossoff took them to a country house with a long wall round it. A gate opened to let them in. Around the house was a large garden.

The visitors washed and had drinks. Kossoff wanted to talk but Holt stopped him. "We can't stay any longer. We must get to the bridge."

"My driver will take you," said Kossoff.

They arrived at the bridge two hours later.

The Khabur was a wide river. The bridge was high enough to let boats go under. It looked bright in the sunlight. There were buildings for the workmen beside it.

Holt spoke to a workman passing by. "Where can I find the Chief Engineer, Mr Scott?"

The man showed them a building by the bridge. "Mr Scott works in there."

"We're also looking for Hassan, the son of Sheik Rahman," said Bill.

"He's at work on the bridge," said the man. "I'm going there now. I'll take you."

"You go and see that Hassan is all right," said Holt to Bill. "I'll speak to Scott."

Bill went off towards the bridge with the workman. Holt went into the Chief Engineer's building.

Scott was a tall man, very thin, with a sad-looking face. "Sheik Rahman told me you were coming," he said.

"You know why?"

"Yes."

"How is Hassan?"

"He's doing very well. He spent two days looking at the plans of the bridge. I think he understands them."

"Have any strangers been here, looking for him?"

"I've not seen any," said Scott.

"You know what happened in England?"

"Yes. But I think it was only a game. Two friends of his from the school, perhaps."

"That was no game," said Holt. "And they weren't a bit friendly."

Bill crossed the bridge with the workman.

"I like your bridge," said Bill.

"It *looks* all right," said the workman. "But some of us aren't happy about it."

"Oh? Why not?"

"It has taken a long time to build. Things are always going wrong."

"That often happens in building."

"Here it happens too often. We've talked to Mr Scott about it. But he doesn't do anything."

They reached the middle of the bridge. The workman called to a friend. "Where's Hassan?"

The other man came over to them. "He's gone. He left the bridge about an hour ago."

"Where did he go?" asked Bill.

"He went away with two men."

"Two men? Who were they?"

"I don't know. I haven't seen them before. They came to the bridge and said they wanted to see Hassan. He went to speak to them. After a while they all got into a car and went off."

"These men," said Bill. "What did they look like?"

"One of them was tall. He had long, black hair. The other man was shorter, but heavy."

"I think I know who they are," said Bill slowly.

Chapter 4

Holt came from the building as Bill ran from the bridge. "I think they've got Hassan," said Bill.

Holt telephoned to Captain Salem. An hour later police were out all over the country, looking for Hassan.

Bill questioned the men on the bridge, one after another. They couldn't help.

Holt talked to Scott again. "We think those men have taken Hassan away."

"You mean, kidnapped him?" said Scott. "I don't believe it. Hassan has lots of friends. Two of them came to see him. He's gone away with them, that's all."

"Without telling you?"

"Young men are like that. He'll come back one day."

Days passed and Hassan did not come back. The police could not find him. And there was no word from the kidnappers.

"I don't understand it," said Holt. "Why don't they ask his father for money?"

"Perhaps it's not money they want," said Bill.

"Not money? What else could they want?"

"I don't know."

A telephone call came for Holt. It was from Scott.

"Hassan is all right, Inspector," said Scott. "I've had a call from him. He's in Cairo with some friends. He'll be back in two weeks."

Holt went to Sheik Rahman's house. The Sheik sat in his garden. His eyes were heavy for want of sleep. Holt told him about the call from Scott.

"Hassan in Cairo?" said the Sheik. "It can't be true. Hassan wouldn't go away like that. He wouldn't leave his work. He wouldn't hurt me in this way. Why does he tell only Scott? No, no. It's all wrong. My son is in great danger, Inspector. I know it!"

Holt went back to the hotel. He walked up and down his room. Bill sat in an armchair.

"Let's suppose that Sheik Rahman is right," said Holt. "Suppose Hassan is not in Cairo. Then those men are still holding him. Did he telephone Scott?"

"Perhaps he didn't," said Bill. "Perhaps there was no call. Scott only said that to stop us looking for Hassan."

"Which means....?"

"That Scott is working with the kidnappers."

"Right!" said Holt.

"How can we find out?"

"One of us must go to the bridge," said Holt. "He must dress like a workman, so Scott won't know him."

"One of us?"

"You or me."

"Scott has seen you," said Bill. "He hasn't seen me. And how can you look like one of these workmen? With that white face of yours?"

"I didn't think of that," said Holt.

"Yes, you did!" said Bill, smiling. "You want me to do it!"

It was early morning. The cleaners were at work in the engineer's building. Bill came in, dressed

like the other cleaners.

"Who are you?" asked one of them.

"My name is Njuko," said Bill. "I've come to work here."

"Oh, all right," said the man. "Get some soap and water."

Bill went to Scott's room, but he didn't clean the floor. He went to the desk. He looked at papers, notes and plans but they told him nothing.

Then he heard voices. He got down on the floor with the soap.

"I want my car at eleven." It was Scott. He came in with another man.

"Where are you going?" asked the man.

"That's not your business," said Scott. "See that the car is ready with a driver." The man went out. Scott saw Bill on the floor. "What are you doing here? Cleaning is finished now. Get out."

At eleven that morning a car stood outside the building. A driver sat in front. Scott got into the back. "Go to the road and turn left," he said.

The car moved off. The driver was Bill.

Chapter 5

Bill drove down the road towards the mountains.

"Turn right here," said Scott. Bill turned the car into a road on the right. "You see that big gate. Drive in there."

Bill drove through the gate. He knew where he was. It was Vladimir Kossoff's house.

He began to think fast: "Kossoff was there when that lorry ran into our car. He brought us here. He kept us here an hour or more – while those men kidnapped Hassan. Now Scott has come to see him. Are Scott and Kossoff working together? Is it all part of a plan?"

"Wait for me," said Scott as he went into the house.

Bill got out of the car. He went round the side of the house. Men were at work there, building a new swimming pool. They did not speak to Bill. He went on, round the back of the house. There were tall windows at the back. Through the windows Bill could see Scott and Kossoff. Both men smiled

as they talked.

"Their plan is going well," thought Bill.

He wanted very much to hear what they said. He couldn't go closer or they would see him. He went back to the front of the house. The door was open and he went in.

Bill heard voices in a room nearby. He walked past the door quietly. He stopped at another door at the back of the house. He could hear voices again. This time it was Kossoff and Scott. Bill put his ear to the door.

He heard Scott saying, "You mustn't kill him."

"We shan't kill him," answered Kossoff. "Not if all goes well. If things go wrong, that's different."

"Nothing can go wrong now," said Scott.

"When will the first train go over the bridge?"

"Next Thursday. It will be a big day. All the top men of the railway will ride on the train."

"Good," said Kossoff. "We'll see what happens. If things go right I'll let the boy go. And you'll have your money."

Just then a man came out of the front room. He saw Bill and called out, "Hi! Who are you? What are you doing here?"

Two more men came from the room. Bill looked round. The only way out was the front door. The three men stood in his way. The first man came towards him.

"I'm looking for the kitchen," said Bill.

"I don't believe you."

"All right," said Bill, "don't believe me!"

He shot out a fist into the man's face. The first man fell back into the arms of the second man. The third one jumped on to Bill. Bill took hold of his arm and turned it round. The man fell to the floor head first and stayed there.

The second man took out a gun. Bill's foot came up and the gun went flying. The man ran back afraid.

That left the first man.

He ran at Bill with his fists up. Bill put his head down and banged it into the man's middle. He went over with a loud cry.

Kossoff and Scott came from the back room. Bill didn't wait for them. He ran out of the house and jumped into the car. As he drove off Kossoff came from the house, calling loudly.

A man stood near the gate. When he heard Kossoff he ran to the gate and began to close it. The gate was heavy. It was half-way shut when Bill reached it. The man jumped back. Bill drove on. The car banged on to the gate and the wall. But it got through!

Bill drove off down the road, fast.

Chapter 6

Bill drove back to the city. He told Holt about his visit to Kossoff's house. They went to see Captain Salem.

"Who is this man, Kossoff?" asked Holt.

"Kossoff is a businessman," said Salem. "He has buses and lorries. A great many of them."

"Was it one of his lorries that ran into our car?" asked Bill.

"That could be. They run from the mountains to the city and back. They carry a lot of people, and most other things too."

"What will happen when the railway is working?" asked Holt. "Won't Kossoff lose his business?"

"Yes, he will. Perhaps he'll go to another country, and start again."

"He's not going to another country," said Bill. "He thinks he's staying here."

"How do you know?" asked Salem.

"He's building a new swimming pool in his

garden."

"That's very strange."

"We must find out what Kossoff and Scott are planning," said Holt. "But first we must find Hassan."

"I think Kossoff is holding him," said Bill. "The question is, where?"

"Shall I send men to Kossoff's house?" asked Salem.

"That won't help," said Holt. "Kossoff won't keep Hassan in his house. If we question him he won't talk."

"Then how can we find Hassan?"

Holt thought for a while. "Send a few men to the house. But tell them to hide so Kossoff won't know. They can keep a look-out. If people leave the house your men can follow them."

"Very well," said Salem.

"One other thing," said Bill. "Before we find Hassan.... *don't send a train over that bridge.*"

Holt and Bill went back to the hotel. On Wednesday morning there was a telephone call from Salem.

"I've had a radio call," he said, "from my men at Kossoff's house. Early this morning two men came to the house in a car. They stayed for an hour. Then they drove into the hills. My men followed them. They went into a cave of some kind. My men are outside the cave. I've told them

to do nothing before we get there."

"Good," said Holt. "We'll go at once."

Salem brought a car. He drove fast into the hills with Holt and Bill. They turned down a small road. When that came to an end they left the car and walked. They found the policemen hidden near the cave.

"Kossoff's men are still in there," said one.

"Shall we go in?" said Salem.

"Yes," said Holt. "But we must go softly. Let me go first. Give me a gun, please." Salem gave Holt a gun. "Wait two minutes. Then you follow."

Holt went into the cave. He walked slowly. It grew very dark. He put a hand on the wall to find his way. Then he saw a light far down the cave. He walked very quietly now, close to the wall.

At the end of the cave there was a bigger space, with a fire burning. Two men sat in front of the fire. One was tall with long black hair. The other was shorter but heavily built. The kidnappers!

The tall man heard Holt's foot on the ground. He turned with a cry and both men jumped up. Then they saw the gun.

"Stay where you are," said Holt.

"Inspector! It's you!" said a voice.

It was Hassan. He sat at the other side of the fire. His hands and feet were held together.

"It's me," said Holt. "Pleased to meet you again."

Chapter 7

The other policemen came to the end of the cave. Bill went to help Hassan.

Salem asked the kidnappers, "Who paid you to do this?"

"We're not getting any pay," said the tall man.

"I think you are," said Salem. "Vladimir Kossoff is paying you."

"Who is he?" asked the short man. "We don't know him."

"You do know him. You came here from his house."

"We stopped at a house to ask for water, for our car. That's all."

"Why were you there for an hour?"

The man didn't answer.

"Take them away," said Salem. "I'll question them again later."

The police took the two men away.

"They won't talk," said Holt. "They're afraid of Kossoff." He turned to Hassan. "How did you get here?"

"They asked for me at the bridge. I went to speak to them. The tall one had a gun under his coat. They made me go with them. They brought me here."

"Do you know why they kidnapped you?"

"To get money from my father, I suppose."

"I think not," said Holt.

"Tell us about the bridge," said Bill.

"The bridge?"

"You looked at the plans and you looked at the bridge. What did you find?"

"There's a lot wrong with it," said Hassan. "It's the middle part that's wrong. The pieces are not put together the right way."

"How bad is it?"

"Very bad. It'll fall down when a train goes over it."

"Just what I thought," said Bill.

"I tried to tell Mr Scott, but he wouldn't listen. I was going to tell my father but those men came."

"That's why they took you away," said Holt. "To keep your mouth shut."

"Kossoff is behind all this," said Bill. "And Scott is working with him. How can we make them talk?"

"There is one way," said Holt. "It won't be easy, but we must try it...."

That afternoon Kossoff stood by his new swimming pool. It was almost finished. Soon he would swim in it.

"Good afternoon, Mr Kossoff."

Holt and Salem came towards the pool.

"What do you want?" asked Kossoff.

"We're sending a train over the Khabur Bridge today," said Holt.

"Today?"

"Yes. Captain Salem and I will go with it."

"I hope you'll like the ride," said Kossoff.

"I hope you will like it too," said Holt.

"Me?"

"Yes. You're coming with us, on the train. Mr Scott is coming too."

Kossoff moved back. "No! No, thank you. I don't like trains." He looked towards the house.

"Don't call your men," said Salem. "My men are here too. All round the house. Shall we go?"

The train was ready to leave. It was small, an engine with one car behind. Salem and Holt arrived with Kossoff and Scott. Policemen were standing nearby.

"Get in, please," said Salem.

Kossoff and Scott looked at the policemen and got on to the train. Holt and Salem climbed in after them.

"Aren't there more people coming?" asked Kossoff.

"No," said Holt. "Only the four of us today.

And the driver, of course."

"I don't want to go...." Scott began.

"Sit down," said Salem.

Bill Ojo stood beside the driver at the front of the engine. "Have I got it right?" he asked. "I take this handle back to go faster? I bring it towards me to slow down?"

"That's right," said the driver.

"I can do it," said Bill. "You can go."

The driver climbed down from the engine. Bill put the handle back slowly. The train began to move.

Chapter 8

"We shall reach the bridge in five minutes," said Holt. He looked at Kossoff. "Why don't you like trains?"

Kossoff said nothing. He sat with his hands together, not moving.

Salem looked out of the window. "I can see the bridge now."

"Four minutes," said Holt.

Scott spoke suddenly. His face was very white. "Stop the train!"

"Stop it? Why?" asked Salem.

"I'm not well. I want to get out."

"We'll stop soon," said Salem. "The other side of the bridge."

"No!" said Scott. "We can't go over the bridge."

"Why not? You must tell us why not."

Scott did not answer.

"Three minutes to go," said Holt.

Scott cried out. "It's the bridge. It's not...."

"Keep your mouth shut!" said Kossoff loudly.

"I can't. I won't. If we go over the bridge we shall all die."

"Why?" asked Salem again, quietly.

"Because...."

"Be quiet!" said Kossoff.

"I won't be quiet. The bridge isn't strong enough. It won't carry a train."

"How do you know that?" asked Holt.

"I know because I built it."

"Do you mean, you *wanted* the bridge to fall?"

"Yes, yes. When the first train went over it. Tomorrow. With the top railway men in it."

"Did you want to kill them all?"

Scott shot a look at Kossoff. "He wanted it. He paid me to do it."

"It's not true," said Kossoff.

"It is true," Scott went on. "He wanted to stop

the railway working. So that he could keep his business. You must believe me."

"I do believe you," said Holt. "Thank you. That's all we wanted to know."

The train was close to the bridge. Bill brought the engine handle towards him. The train began to slow down.

Salem spoke to Scott and Kossoff. "We're stopping now. You'll both come with me and...."

Kossoff jumped to his feet. "No! You won't get me!"

Before they could stop him he ran down the car. He went through the door at the end, into the engine car. Salem ran after him but the door closed in his face. It wouldn't open again.

The train came to a stop just in front of the bridge. Holt climbed down from the car, on to the ground. Salem and Scott followed him.

Bill opened the side door at the front of the engine. He was going to jump down. Suddenly the door from the car opened. Kossoff came through it. He ran to the other side, his only way of escape.

"Hi! Stop!" cried Bill.

He ran across and got hold of Kossoff. The big man turned fast. He put a fist into Bill's face. Bill fell back, still holding on to Kossoff. The two went over together. They fell on to the engine handle....

The train began to move again. It ran on to the bridge, slowly at first, then faster.

Holt and the others were beside it. "Bill! Look

out!" called Holt.

There was nothing Bill could do. He was on the floor of the car. Kossoff was on top of him. Kossoff jumped up. He tried again to reach the side door. Bill got hold of his legs. They fought again.

The train reached the middle of the bridge. There was a loud noise, like a thousand windows breaking. Pieces of the bridge rained down into the river. The train began to fall, engine first.

The two men fell away from each other. Bill went head first out of the side door. Kossoff fell back through the door behind, into the engine space.

Holt and the others saw the bridge break up. They saw the train fall like a stone. Scott put his hands over his eyes. The river closed over the train. Soon there were only broken bits of wood on top of the water.

For a little while there was nothing more. Then a head came up. Only one head, not two.

"Hi! Hi, there!" called Holt.

A dark face turned towards them in the water. It was Bill Ojo.

"I can't thank you enough," said Sheik Rahman.

"Same here," said Hassan.

"I'm sorry about the bridge," said Holt.

"We shall build the bridge again. Kossoff will help to pay for it."

"But Kossoff is dead," said Bill.

"Yes, but we shall take his money. He can still pay for what he did." The Sheik smiled at Hassan. "Next time my son will be there."

"We know one thing now," said Holt. "Hassan is a good engineer."

A Word Game

Do you like word games? Try this one. We've written 36 sentences about the story. Some of these sentences are *true,* and some are *not true.* Look at the two letters at the end of every sentence. When the sentence is *true,* write down the FIRST LETTER. When the sentence is *not true,* write down the SECOND LETTER.

Put every letter at its number here (they make a German saying):

__ __ __ __ __ __ __ __ __ __ __ __ __ __
1 2 3 4 5 6 7 8 9 10 11 12 13 14

__ __ __ __ __ S __ __ __ __ __ E __ __ __
15 16 17 18 19   20 21 22 23 24   25 26 27

__ __ __ __ __ __ __ __ E __
28 29 30 31 32 33 34 35   36

1 In England, two men took Hassan away in a black car. (D,I)
2 Sheik Rahman was not a poor man. (T,O)
3 The kidnappers put a coat over Hassan's head. (I,N)
4 Holt was the driver of the police car. (T,S)
5 The Khabur Bridge was in the Middle East. (A,C)
6 Sheik Rahman was Hassan's uncle. (R,B)
7 Ahmed took Inspector Holt from the airport to a restaurant. (O,A)
8 Sheik Rahman paid for the hotel rooms. (D,S)

9 The railways went from the mountains to the sea. (B,S)
10 The railway crossed the Khabur Road. (Y,R)
11 A thief took Holt's money from the hotel room. (O,I)
12 A lorry crashed into Sheik Rahman's car. (D,U)
13 Sheik Rahman's house was in the mountains. (R,G)
14 Kossoff drove Bill and Inspector Holt to the bridge. (B,E)
15 The kidnappers asked Hassan's father for money. (R,T)
16 Boats could go under the Khabur Bridge. (H,I)
17 Scott said Hassan was in Cairo. (A,D)
18 Inspector Holt dressed as a cleaner. (G,T)
19 Bill looked at the papers in Scott's office. (I,E)
20 Ahmed drove Scott to Kossoff's house. (B,S)
21 Kossoff was building a new swimming pool. (H,E)
22 Holt went into the cave without a gun. (F,O)
23 The kidnappers hid in a cave. (R,O)
24 Hassan was not in the cave. (R,T)
25 Kossoff had many buses and lorries. (R,Y)
26 The end part of the bridge was wrong. (O,T)
27 The driver left the train before it moved off. (H,U)
28 The train had an engine and a few cars. (C,A)
29 Inspector Holt drove the train. (O,N)

30 The train took half an hour to reach the bridge. (M,T)
31 Kossoff said, "Stop the train!" (E,H)
32 The bridge was not strong enough for a train. (E,T)
33 Scott and Bill fell in the river. (O,R)
34 Salem was an engineer. (T,I)
35 Bill drove Scott to Kossoff's house. (V,H)
36 Kossoff paid Scott to stop the railway. (R,M)

But you haven't finished yet!
You haven't used all the letters. Write those other letters at their number here (they make an English saying):

```
__ __ __ __ __ __ __ __ __ __ __ __ __ __
 1  2  3  4  5  6  7  8  9 10 11 12 13 14

__ __ __ __ __ S __ __ __ __ __ E __ __ __
15 16 17 18 19   20 21 22 23 24   25 26 27

__ __ __ __ __ __ __ __ E __
28 29 30 31 32 33 34 35   36
```

Answers

The others are not true.
36.
2, 3, 5, 8, 9, 12, 16, 17, 19, 21, 23, 25, 27, 32, 35,
These sentences are true:

48

Collins English Library
LEVEL 2

THE BRIDGE

Days passed and Hassan did not come back. The police could not find him. And there was no word from the kidnappers.

"I don't understand it," said Holt. "Why don't they ask his father for money?"

"Perhaps it's not money they want," said Bill. "Not money? What else could they want?"

Why do two men kidnap a Sheik's son if they do not want money? It is very strange.
This story takes Inspector Holt and Bill Ojo to the Middle East to find the kidnappers.

0 00 370126 3

A Collins Graded Reader